This edition published by Parragon Books Ltd in 2014

Parragon Books Ltd
Chartist House
15–17 Trim Street
Bath BA1 1HA, UK
www.parragon.com

Written by Frances Prior-Reeves
Designed by Talking Design
Illustrations by Carol Seatory

ISBN 978-1-4723-5623-9

Printed in China

Doodles of Fun!

PaRragon

Bath • New York • Cologne • Melbourne • Delhi
Hong Kong • Shenzhen • Singapore • Amsterdam

Fill this window box with
flowers.

Fill this page with
cubes.

**Can you build an object
from those cubes?**

Design these
bags.

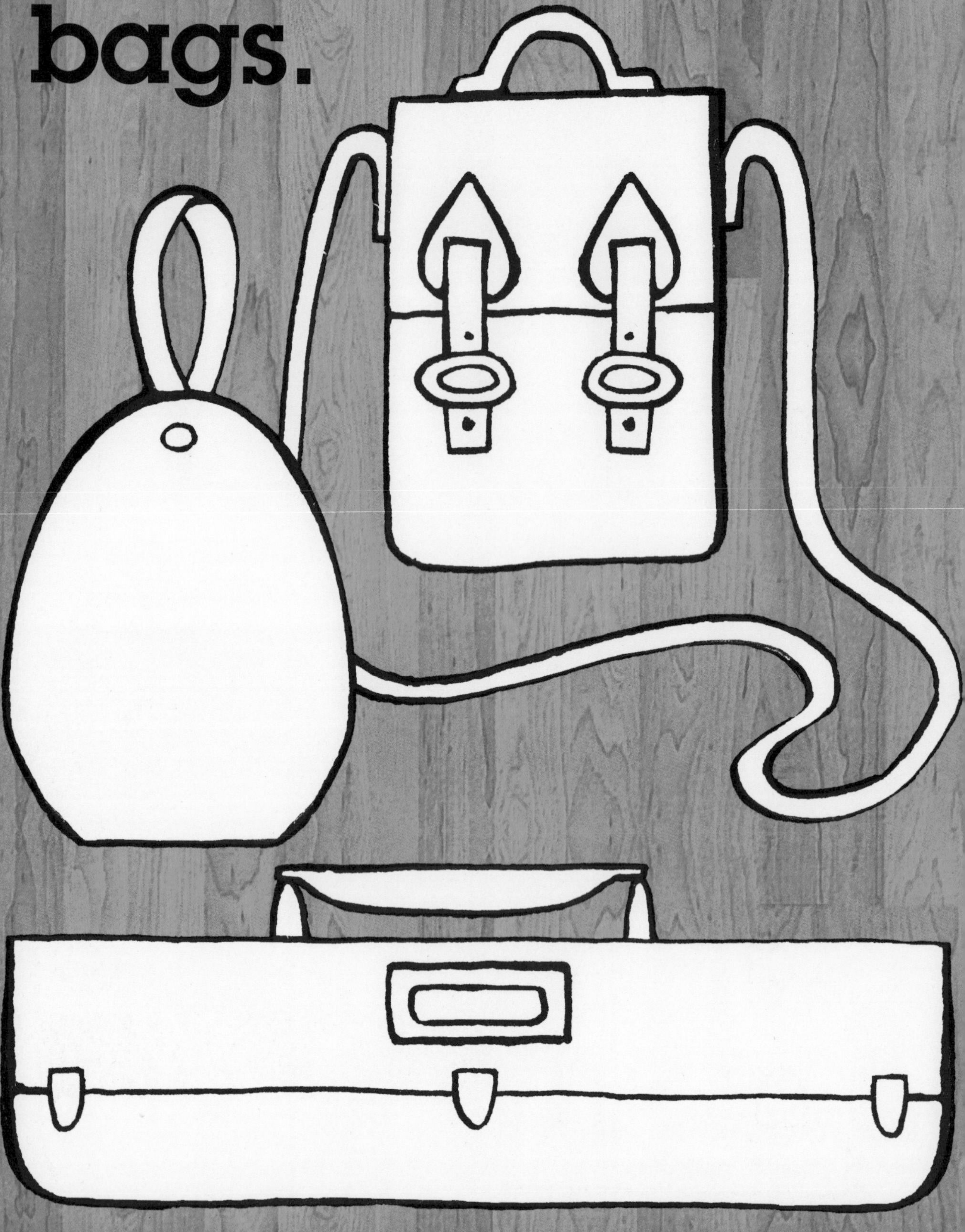

Fill this jar

with candy canes.

Space for you
to doodle.

Draw the other half of
this owl.

Draw your favourite
animals
in this field altogether.

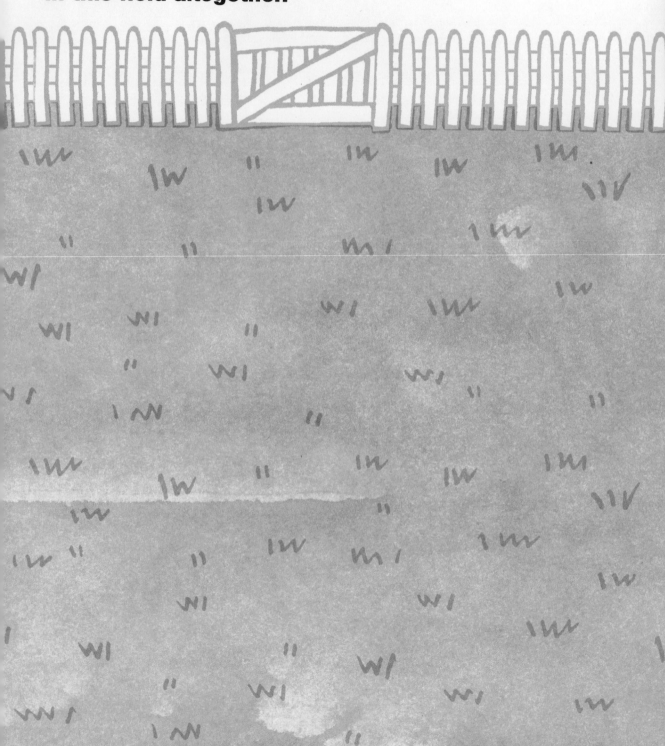

Do they all get along or do you need to draw a divide?

Draw...

a **pirate**,

a **queen**

and a
magician.

Now draw **one image** of all three.

Colour these patterns.

Wrap this gift.

Unwrap

this present in the space above, what is it?

Draw a monster

with two heads, three eyes, five arms and one mouth.

Decorate
this room for a birthday party.

Draw the

autumn leaves

falling from this tree.

Draw a playground

for your parents.

Scribble in colour.

Add some colourful
wellies
splashing in these puddles.

Fill this sky with **kites.**

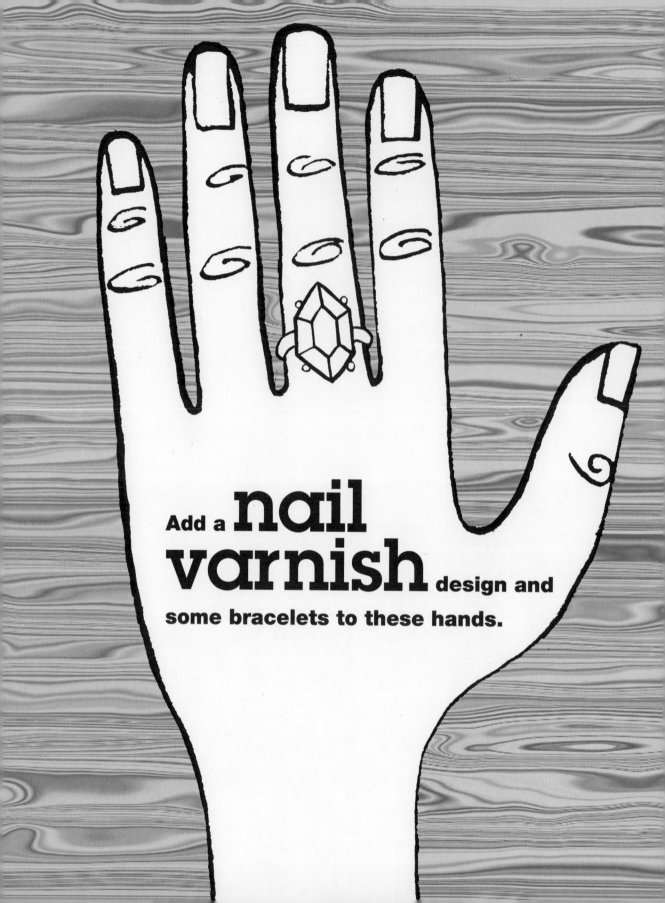

Add a **nail varnish** design and some bracelets to these hands.

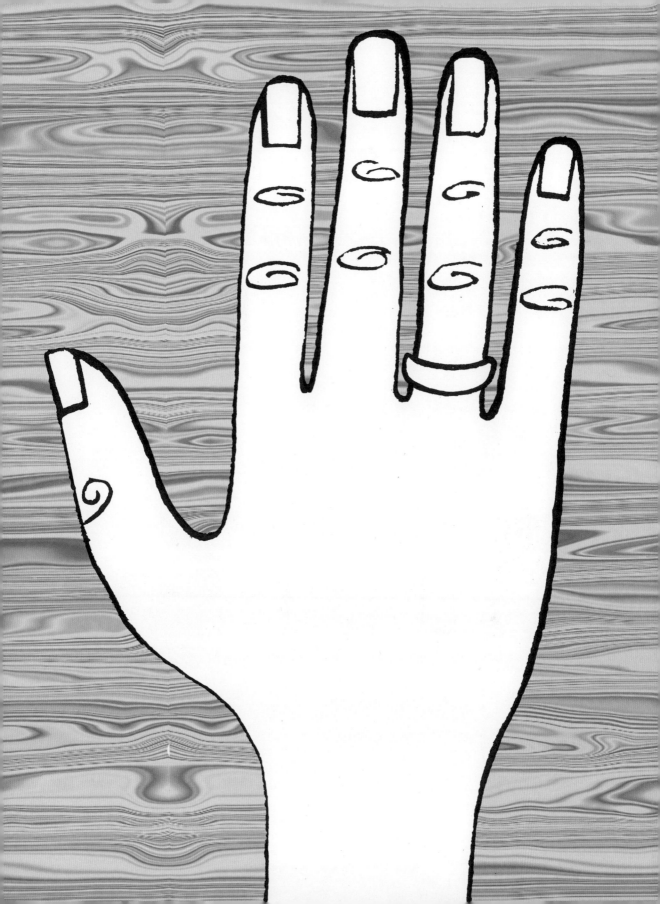

Fill these frames with postmodern art.

Draw something you love using only heart shapes.

Draw an
octopus
having a fight with a
spider.

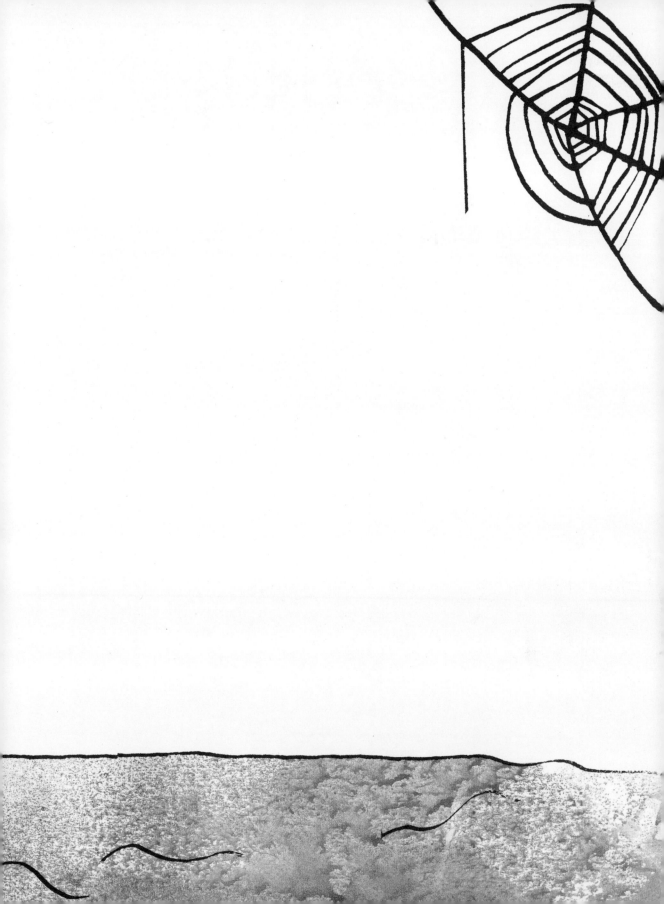

Draw **sandcastles** on this beach.

Draw **yourself**

with your eyes closed.

Draw
yourself
on your head.

Doodle!

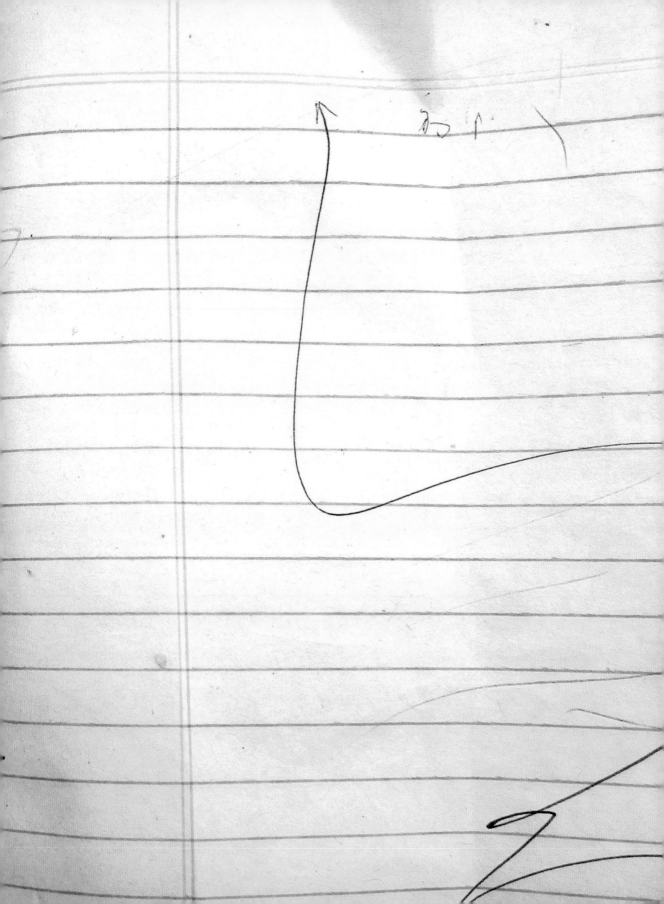

Fill this page with
triangles.

Can you turn those triangles into
butterflies?

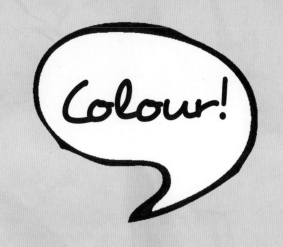

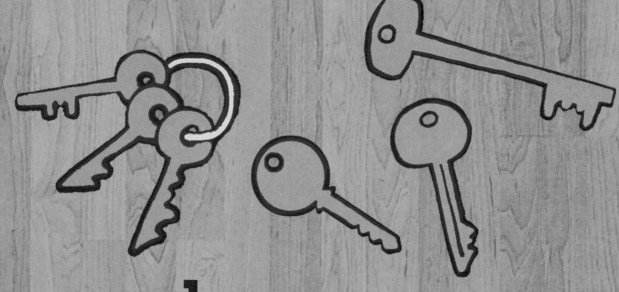

Fill this jar with **keys.**

Turn these shapes into
insects.

Draw the other half of this
hot-air
balloon.

Draw some more
passengers ✓
in the basket.

Space for you to be creative.

Draw a galaxy full of stars.

Create a pattern using
spirals.

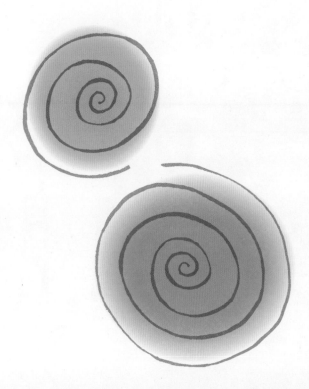

Make this house
haunted.

Draw your favourite thing
using only your favourite colour.

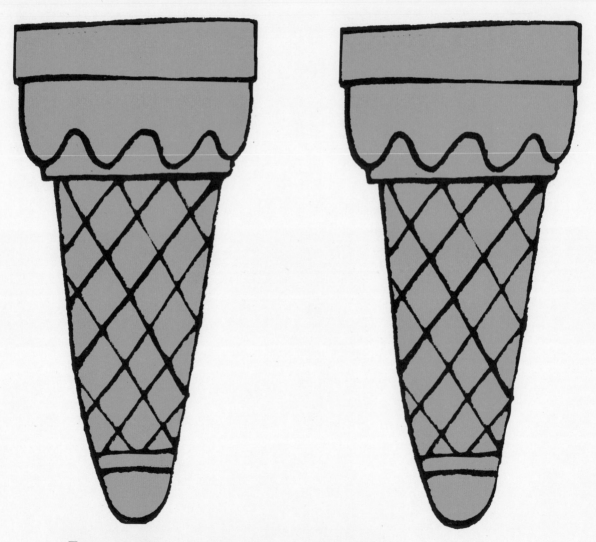

Add **ice cream** to these cones.

Doodle, colour, shade or scribble anything.

Create a colourful **pattern**
using this graph paper.

Draw the other half of this
dragon.

Draw some people queuing for the sale which starts tomorrow.

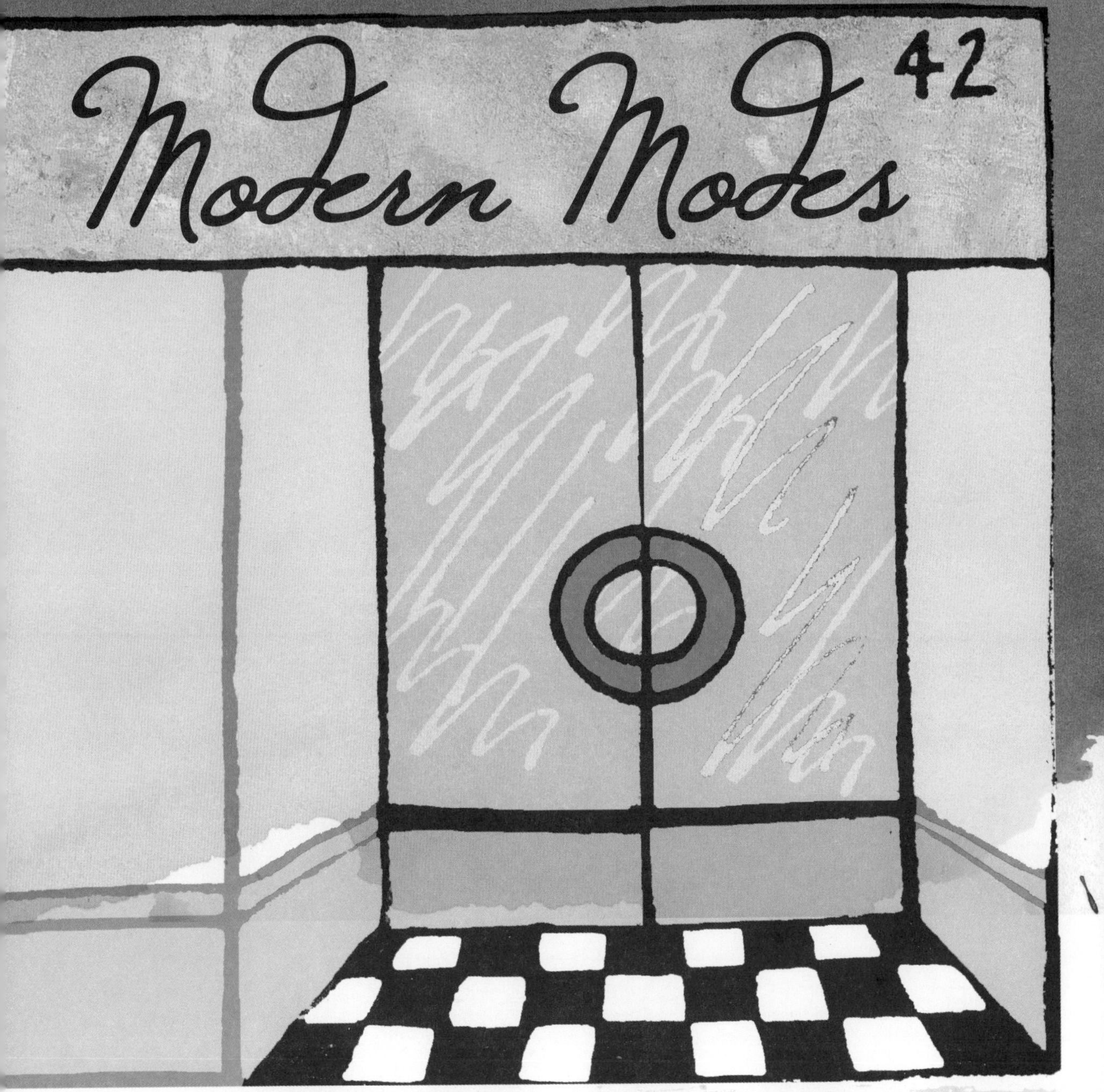
Modern Modes 42

Draw **wings** for yourself and your best friend and **fly away.**

Draw a house
using only circles.

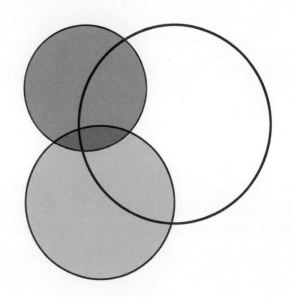

Add bees to this beehive.

Plant flowers

for these bees.

Create a pattern using only
the letters from your name, over and over.

Fill this **seabed** with things that can **swim.**

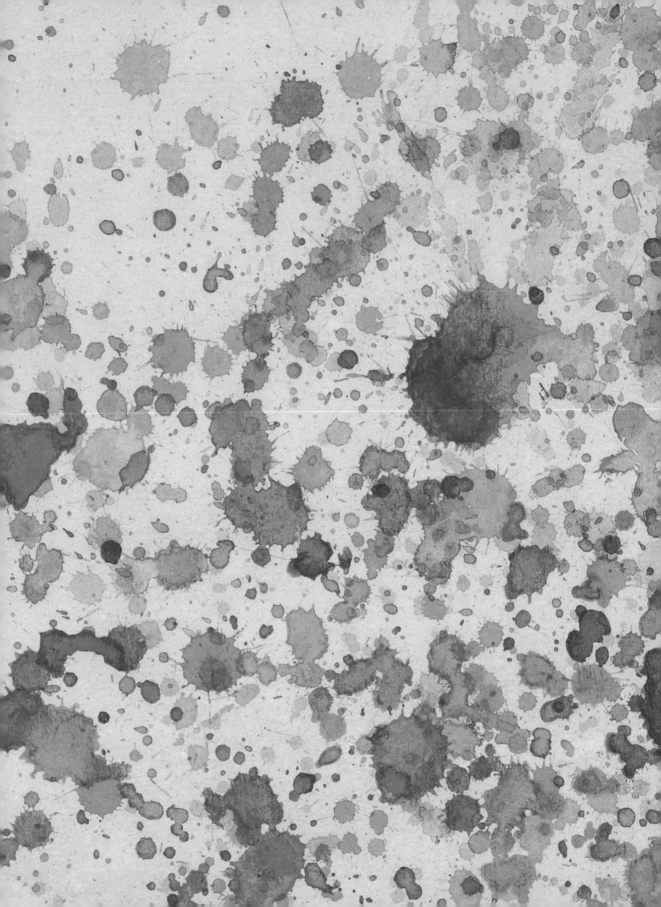

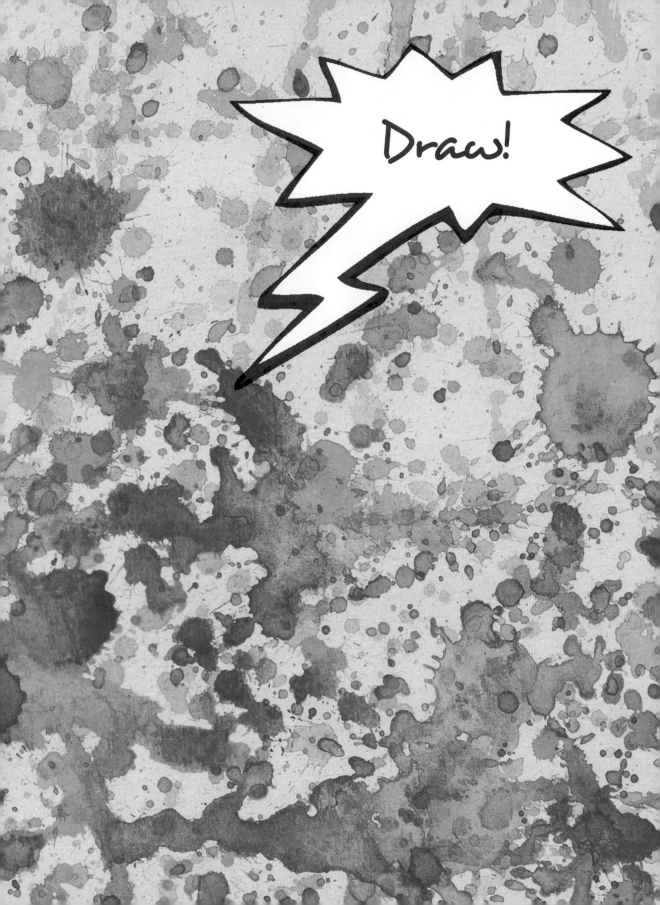

Design these **curtains.**

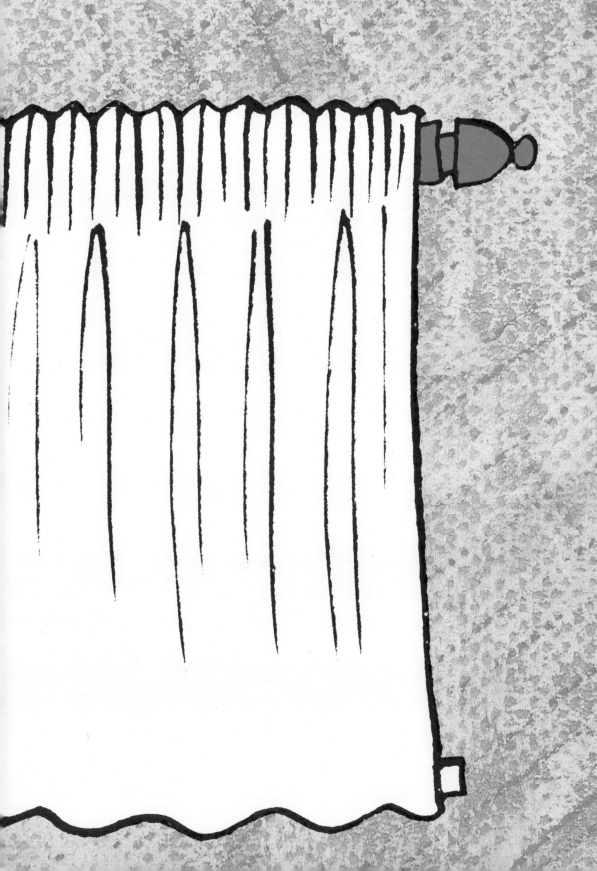

Draw a **bicycle** for this dog.

Colour in these **patterns.**

Spread your **favourite toppings** on these bagels.

Fill this page with animals that come

out in the daytime**.**

Fill this page with animals that come out at **night-time.**

Colour these
high heels.

Now design your own shoes.

Oodles of doodles!

Draw...

ₐdonkey,

ₐbear